Alien Abduction

Andrew Donkin

For Emma

Keep watching the skies!

Andrew
Donk

Bloomsbury

ACKNOWLEDGEMENTS

My grateful thanks to all the many investigators, researchers and witnesses who have contributed to the UFO and abduction debate over the last half a century. Especially, Budd Hopkins, John Mack, Jenny Randles and Whitley Strieber.

Special thanks must go to UFOlogist Lorne Mason, who generously opened his own personal X-Files to help with the writing of this book.

Thanks also to Andrew Collins for ten years of good ideas; Barry Cunningham for setting the ball rolling. And a tip of the hat to Ron Fogelman, Jamie Finch, and Sophie Hicks for their input.

Finally, and most importantly, a huge thank you for all her help and much, much love to Suzy Jenvey.

———

First published in Great Britain in 1997
Bloomsbury Publishing Plc, 38 Soho Square, London W1V 5DF

A CIP catalogue record of this book is available from the British Library

ISBN 0 7475 3147 1

Text design by AB3.
Printed and bound in Great Britain by
Cox & Wyman Limited, Reading, Berkshire.

10 9 8 7 6 5 4 3 2 1

Contents

CHAPTER 1

They're Here

DATELINE: Now
LOCATION: Earth

File No: 4385-67
Dateline: 11 October, 1973
Location: Pascagoula River, Mississippi, USA

Charles Hickson and Calvin Parker were
abducted while night-fishing for catfish on
the Pascagoula River, Mississippi. An oval
object flew down and hovered over the river
just metres away from the watching men.
Three humanoid creatures with slit eyes
floated out of the craft. The men were
carried inside the brightly lit ship where
they were quickly examined before being
returned to the riverside. Other fishermen
witnessed the UFO leaving and later both men
passed lie detector tests.

File No: 6529-77
Dateline: 27 October, 1974
Location: Aveley, Essex, England

The Avis family were driving home late at
night through the English countryside when
they saw a bright blue light in the sky that
seemed to keep pace with their car. As they
drove into a bank of thick green mist that
covered the road their car stalled. Hypnosis

later revealed they were taken onboard a
UFO. Inside the craft were two different
species of aliens: one tall and humanoid,
the other small, ugly and hairy. They
studied the family before placing them back
in their car.

File No: 9732-04
Dateline: 30 November, 1989
Location: New York, USA

Linda Cortile was asleep in her bed when she
became aware that they had come back. For
years the small grey aliens had been regular
but uninvited visitors into her Manhattan
apartment. Linda tried to get away from
them, but she was paralysed. Linda found
herself being floated towards a spacecraft
hovering over the rooftop. Inside the ship,

she was looked over and examined by the creatures. What scared her most was their huge black eyes 'that never, ever blink'. In the morning, she awoke exhausted back in her own bed.

Extraordinarily, this abduction was also witnessed by two other people. On the street below, a pair of New York police officers had seen the woman floated out of her building. They had seen the spacecraft. And they had seen its occupants.

THEY'RE HERE!

These are just a few of hundreds of similar reports from all around the world that claim that alien creatures are regularly visiting our planet and abducting (or spacenapping as it is sometimes called) human beings.

Over the last few decades the number of reports like these has grown from a few odd cases into a flood of stories from credible witnesses.

The people making these extraordinary claims are rational and normal individuals. They do not want fame and they are not attempting to make money; in many cases they do not even want their identity to be publicly known.

WEIRD CREATURES

The experiences that the abductees report range from the terrifying to the bizarre and wonderful.

Typically, most experiences occur at night when the abductee wakes in bed to see a bright light or strange glow shining through their bedroom window. Strange figures then seem to emerge from out of the light.

The alien creatures encountered vary from report to

report, but one of the most commonly seen types is 'the Greys'. These small beings are usually one metre or so tall with large heads and big black eyes. The Greys get their name from the pale silver colour of their skin.

The witness is floated up and out of bed, often passing through solid objects like a closed window or the ceiling of the room.

Once on board the spacecraft, the abductee is usually examined by aliens acting like doctors.

Sometimes the alien entities give the witness a message or warning, often to do with ecology and pollution. They explain that humankind is destroying the planet Earth and that if it does not stop wasting the Earth's resources then the planet will not survive.

The abductee is then returned to their bed where they wake next morning. In some cases they have a conscious memory of the abduction events, in others they are only aware of missing time or of having had vivid and terrifying nightmares. It may take a session (or several) of hypnosis to recover the memories of what actually happened.

The second most common abduction scenario is of an individual taken from their car. Invariably they are driving through the countryside at night, a light is seen in the sky following the vehicle and as it gets nearer, the car engine may stall, bringing the car to a halt.

The driver wakes later in the night to find themselves sitting back at the wheel of their car. They complete their journey, but when they reach their destination it is hours later than it should be.

THE EXPERTS SPEAK

UFOlogist and abduction expert, Lorne Mason, has made a study of these strange incidents for over a decade: 'The thing that really makes you sit up and take notice of abduction reports is the number of people who tell the same story. Different people from different countries are all having the same experience.'

While researching UFO and abduction cases Mason keeps an open mind but says: 'When you have a teacher from New York reporting exactly the same events as a farmer from Mexico, or a medicine man in Africa, you have to take it seriously.'

Recently John E. Mack, a professor at Harvard Medical School, published the results of his studies of nearly one hundred abductees. Mack began the investigation feeling sceptical, but towards the end concluded: 'The experimental data, which is the most important information that we have, suggests that abductees have been visited by some sort of "alien" intelligence.'

His book unleashed a storm of controversy that a respected Harvard professor should express such an opinion.

Abduction reports lack the kind of hard physical evidence that it would take to convince real sceptics as there are rarely any photographs or burn marks and usually no other witnesses apart from the abductee.

However, if these witnesses were reporting almost anything other than visitations from alien beings then they would be believed without question.

If they were reporting a crime then the detail and clarity of their memories would leave most people in little doubt as to what they had seen. Because alien abductions go against the grain of current scientific thinking, the experiences are often dismissed as nightmares or other sleep-related trauma.

Reports of alien abductions continue to come in from all around the globe. The vast majority of them are normal everyday people telling remarkable and sometimes frightening stories.

Whether you believe the witnesses or not ... something is happening out there. These are their stories ...

CHAPTER 2

The Sightings

```
File No: 2000-01
Dateline: 24 June, 1947
Location: Washington State, USA
```

'LIKE A SAUCER'

The modern era of UFOs is generally said to have begun with Kenneth Arnold's now famous sighting over the snow-capped peaks of the Cascade mountains.

Arnold was flying his private plane when he spotted a group of nine objects flying in between the distant mountain peaks. The craft had curved wings and moved by almost bouncing through the air. The nine craft weaved through the white mountain tops, flying in carefully observed formation.

In all the hours spent piloting his plane, Arnold had never seen anything like them before and when he landed he reported what he had seen. Asked to describe the craft he said: 'They moved like a saucer skipping across water'.

Although Kenneth Arnold was talking about the way the strange craft moved, rather than their shape, a journalist covering the story came up with the description: 'Flying Saucer'. The name stuck, and the report made Arnold famous around the world.

File No: 2314-08
Dateline: 2 July, 1947
Location: Roswell, New Mexico, USA

The Roswell Incident is now one of the best known UFO cases in the world.

It began during a night time thunder storm when William 'Mac' Brazel and other members of his family heard a loud explosion near their remote homestead. Next day, Brazel who was a rancher, was out riding on horseback when he came across crash wreckage scattered around a deep gouge ripped into the ground.

Brazel and his companion examined the site and realised that something pretty large had crashed down from the sky. Their first thoughts were that it must have been an Air Force plane.

STRANGE SYMBOLS

As however, they began to find bits of the actual object they became more puzzled because it seemed to be composed of materials that they had never seen before. It was lightweight like cloth, but at the same time it was tough and shiny like metal, and was not even dented by a blow from the family sledgehammer. On some pieces the pair of ranchers could see strange symbols and writing.

Brazel collected some of the debris to show his family. He also reported the crash to the authorities at nearby Roswell Air Force Base.

The officer in charge at the time was Major Jesse Marcel who travelled to the crash site to see the debris for himself. He immediately decided they were very important and ordered a full scale clear up operation by the Air Force. Every single piece of wreckage (including those bits first taken by Brazel) were gathered together and taken away.

A few days later, a press statement was issued confirming that the US Air Force was in possession of the crashed remains of a 'flying disc'. Coming as it did, only a few weeks after Kenneth Arnold's 'Saucer' sighting, this was world-wide news.

GOVERNMENT LIES?

It was after this that many people claim the cover up began. The Air Force seemed to change its mind and put out another statement saying that the debris was just the remains of a weather balloon.

In the years since then, other rumours have begun to circulate. Rumours that the Air Force found not just wreckage, but alien bodies as well. In some versions of events the creatures were alive when they were found by the Air Force, in others they were already dead. The wreckage and the recovered bodies are supposed to be kept at a top security base somewhere in the USA.

For decades investigators have tried to find out the truth about what really crashed at Roswell. Was it an out of control alien spaceship? Or something much more ordinary?

The story was given an interesting twist recently when the US government admitted that they had lied. They said what actually fell from the sky at Roswell was a top secret project designed at the time to spy on the Russians, but many experts dismissed this as yet another red herring.

A REAL LIFE X-FILE

In the last few years, the Roswell Incident has inspired writers to create their own stories based on the recovery of crashed alien spacecraft. The X-Files TV series has included several

Roswell-related episodes including 'Conduit', 'Fallen Angel' and 'Piper Maru'. Roswell also featured as an important part of the blockbuster science fiction film Independence Day.

Footage claiming to show an autopsy performed by doctors on the alien bodies has also been released on video. The distributor claimed that the film dates back to 1947, but most experts suspected that it was little more than a money-making hoax.

It is now fifty years since the incident itself, and as UFOlogist Lorne Mason says: 'The only thing we can be certain of is that there was a crash and afterwards a cover up. However, whether they were hiding a crashed UFO or a secret military aircraft or even a Russian spy plane, we'll probably never know.'

**File No: 2123–44
Dateline: 7 January, 1948
Location: Kentucky, USA**

THE FIRST UFO DEATH

In one of the saddest stories from the saucer age, Captain Thomas Mantell became probably the first UFO fatality.

Captain Mantell and three other pilots were flying their P51 Mustang aircraft on a training exercise when their mission controller radioed and asked them to investigate a UFO sighting near their home base.

The other three pilots broke off the pursuit at various points, but Mantell kept after the craft reporting: 'It appears to be a metallic object, tremendous in size. It's directly ahead and slightly above me. I'm trying to close in for a better look.'

These turned out to be Mantell's last words because only moments later he was dead and wreckage from his plane lay strewn across the ground.

The military authorities came up with an 'official' version of events and said that Captain Mantell had mistaken the planet Venus for a UFO. They claimed he had lost consciousness as he 'chased' it too high.

SEARCHING FOR CLUES

People who knew Mantell as a skilful and professional pilot with over 2,800 hours of flight time found that hard to believe.

This report has a fascinating epilogue because an American film crew have recently recovered buried debris from the crash.

Researchers from the American television show Sightings visited the crash sight with metal detectors and unearthed the remains of some of the aircraft wreckage where it had been buried by the military. The serial numbers on the wreckage matched Mantell's plane exactly.

The fragments were tested and even though they had been buried underground for nearly five decades they registered as having 'strong levels of radiation': a finding that no one has been able to explain.

Sightings of weird objects in the air continued to be reported, but in the 1950s it seemed that the strange craft began to land and witnesses started reporting their first encounters with the bizarre creatures inside them.

File No: 2885-50
Dateline: 12 September, 1952
Location: West Virginia, USA

HIDING IN THE DARK

In West Virginia, USA, a total of seven witnesses (five children and two adults) were scared out of their wits by the appearance of a five-metre-tall alien with bright orange eyes.

The group had gone to investigate what they thought was a fallen meteor, but arriving at the impact site they found a pulsating ball of fire waiting for them instead. Looking around, they soon discovered a huge alien (wearing something like a monk's robes) who was hiding in the darkness of the trees.

The alien's face was a frightening blood-red colour and when it floated towards the group they turned and fled, screaming in terror. Many of the witnesses spent the rest of the evening vomiting which they were certain was caused by breathing in a strange and foul tasting odour that was all around the crash site.

A search by a local newspaper the next day found a perfect circle of crushed grass and soil where the object had been seen. The bad smell lingered around the site for days.

**File No: 3691-21
Dateline: 10 September, 1954
Location: Valenciennes, France**

LOOKING FOR INTRUDERS

Alerted by the barking of his dog, Marius Dewilde stepped outside his home to check for unwelcome intruders. He found them.

To his amazement, there were two very strange creatures loitering by the front of the house. They were only one metre tall and seemed to be wearing diving suits and helmets. The beings had no visible arms and shuffled around on their very short legs.

Behind them, sitting on the railway line near his house, Dewilde could see something that looked like a 'parked' UFO. Dewilde moved closer to the creatures, but a beam of green light shot out of the craft and he found himself unable to move.

The entities fled back to their ship which then rose into the air and left. Marius Dewilde tried to alert the village police, but at first they just ignored his weird story. However he persisted and eventually they agreed to investigate.

UNEXPLAINED MARKS

What they found was quite incredible. Although the entities themselves had left no footprints or other physical evidence, their ship had. Where Dewilde had seen the ship resting on the railway line, it had left marks deeply cut into the wooden railway sleepers.

An engineer from the railway calculated that whatever had caused the marks must have weighted thirty tonnes.

It was later confirmed that other people in the area had reported a strange light moving through the sky just after Dewilde said he had disturbed his weird visitors.

'This is an interesting case,' says Lorne Mason, 'not only is there physical evidence, but also sightings by the other locals who also saw the craft leaving. This sighting was actually just one in a whole wave that was taking place over north-west Europe that year.'

File No: 3745-56
Dateline: 21 August, 1955
Location: Hopkinsville, Kentucky, USA

In 1955 a number of goblin-like aliens lay siege to an entire family for a night. In total there were eleven witnesses to this unique 'contact', if indeed it can be called that.

'ALL THE COLOURS OF THE RAINBOW'

Events began in the early evening of 21 August when Billy Ray Taylor saw a large shining UFO land in a dried-up riverbed near the Sutton Farm. He said that it had an exhaust that emitted 'all the colours of the rainbow'.

He reported what he had seen to the Sutton family waiting inside the farmhouse, but they did not believe him and laughed at his story.

It wasn't long before they stopped laughing. An hour later, the family dog started barking loudly and stepping outside the house to investigate, Lucky Sutton and Billy Ray saw a dome-headed creature approaching them.

The being was about one metre tall with large eyes and big pointed ears. Its body gave off a silver glow and the creature had its hands raised in the air as if in a gesture of surrender.

Ignoring the alien's stance completely, the two men aimed their guns and fired directly at it. The shots hit its body making a sound like 'shooting water in a pail'. The impact of the bullets caused the little being to somersault backwards. It then fled into the safety of the dark.

UNDER SIEGE

That was only the beginning. Several other identical entities surrounded the farmhouse as the Sutton family found themselves trapped in a night of terror.

The being's goblin-like faces would appear at a window and the men would shoot at them from inside the house. The creatures would retreat for a while only to return a short time later. At one point one of the creatures was shot off a tree branch and floated down to Earth before running away.

Eventually the family had had enough and at eleven o'clock they ran to their two cars and fled into the nearest town. They returned in the company of the local police, but there was no sign of any of the creatures or of their ship.

WE'RE BACK!

After the police had left, the family tried to get some sleep, but as family member Glennie Lankford was settling down between her bed covers she spotted a luminous glow coming from her window. Staring through the glass was one of the creatures. They had returned.

She alerted the others and (despite her pleas for a more peaceful approach) once again the men started shooting. The creatures stayed around the house until just before dawn when they disappeared for good after one of the longest Earthbound encounters on record.

Despite the men's trigger happy welcome to Earth, at no time did the creatures attack or threaten the family. Of all the reports detailing encounters with aliens these creatures seemed to be the keenest to make contact.

Perhaps if these little goblin aliens hadn't received such a violent welcome they would have made themselves known to the rest of the world and history would have taken a very different course.

As the 1950s drew on, reports of strange creature emerging from UFOs were filed in countries everywhere. Yet of the dozens of reported cases, no one ever managed to obtain photographic proof or solid evidence of their visitors that would stand up to close examination.

A CASE JUST TOO WEIRD

In 1957 a young man claimed to have had an experience that was totally different from anything that had gone before. In fact, the investigators looking into the case thought that the man's story was so 'wild' that they kept it a closely guarded secret for over three years.

Today, the case would be instantly recognized as a typical alien abduction.

File No: 4129-33
Dateline: 15 October, 1957
Location: Brazil

The witness (or abductee as he would be called now) was a young Brazilian farmer called Antonio Villas Boas. Antonio used to work on his farm land long into the night to avoid the exhausting heat of the daytime sun.

Having seen strange lights in the sky the previous night, Antonio was startled when he spotted a 'large red star' that looked as if it was coming towards him. As the UFO got nearer its brilliance lit up the entire field.

The object landed in front of Antonio, who sat in his tractor, watching transfixed. However when the craft began to extend 'exit legs', it was a different story. Antonio became terrified and tried to drive away, but his tractor engine stopped dead so he climbed out and began to run.

He had not got far across the field when he felt something grab his arm. Four humanoids in weird grey suits took hold of him and began dragging him towards the craft. They wore breathing helmets like underwater divers and each stood about as high as the farmer's shoulder.

IN ALIEN HANDS

Antonio struggled desperately to get away, but he could not escape and eventually the four aliens got him inside their ship. Antonio described the interior as being 'brightly lit metallic rooms'.

His captors began to talk to each other, making sounds that Antonio could only liken to dog's barking. 'Those sounds were so totally different from anything I had ever heard before… I still shudder when I think of them,' he said afterwards.

The aliens then examined and washed him with a clear thick liquid, before taking a sample of his blood.

After a vomiting session caused by exposure to a strange gas, Antonio was introduced to a woman who seemed almost human. It disturbed Antonio when he realised that although she looked human she was only capable of making animal-like grunts.

Antonio was taken on a tour of the alien ship and in one room tried to steal a clock-like device to take back as a keepsake. This idea seemed to really anger his captors. [Maybe they were worried they'd be late for their next abduction without it.]

The farmer was eventually allowed to leave and go back to his field.

A LANDMARK

UFO experts as well as official investigators from the Brazilian military found Antonio to be a credible, stable and sincere witness. He stuck exactly to the details of his fantastic tale whenever he retold it and did so until his death many years later.

'This is a real landmark case,' explains Lorne Mason, 'because it was one of the very first of what we would now call abductions.'

It was indeed one of the first cases, but as we will see it was far from being the last.

CHAPTER 3

The Abductions

File No: 5295-77
Dateline: 19 September, 1961
Location: Indian Head, USA

Barney Hill and his wife, Betty, were on their way home from a holiday when they were abducted in what became one of the best known cases in America.

The couple were driving back from Canada late at night when they spotted a 'star-like light' moving mysteriously across the heavens.

Barney Hill studied the object through binoculars and decided that it was obviously a craft of some kind. He was sure he could see windows in its hull, and even occupants moving around inside. Panicked with the sudden thought that he and his wife were going to be captured, Barney drove away as fast as he could.

ALIEN NIGHTMARES

When the Hills arrived home they found that it was much later than it should have been. They had two hours of missing time to account for.

Suffering from nightmares and other symptoms, the Hills eventually sought help and two years after the encounter, Boston psychiatrist Dr Benjamin Simon used hypnotic regression to attempt to recover the full story.

Hypnotic regression is often used in cases like this one because it can help people recall events that they have no conscious memory about. However, most experts agree that there is no guarantee that 'memories' uncovered by hypnotic regression are accurate memories of real events.

The technique was used on the Hills and the result was a surprise to everyone concerned. The story unfolded like this:

After the Hills had tried to drive away, their car had been stopped by the UFO and the Hills had been floated into the craft.

The occupants, glimpsed earlier, were about one and a half metres tall and had large heads with big curving eyes, very similar in appearance to what would later be called the Greys. The creatures gave the Hills a full medical examination and took skin and blood samples from both of them.

The creatures even showed Betty a star map and explained that it detailed their trading routes between star systems. The couple were then taken back to their car and told to forget what they had seen, before they were allowed to drive home.

Doctor Simon, in charge of the Hill's hypnosis, remained unconvinced by the couple's newly revealed story.

He felt that the things they had 'remembered' under hypnosis were probably just fantasies. Many other investigators, though, did take them seriously.

TRACKED ON RADAR

When evaluating the Hill case two other very important factors need to be kept in mind.

First, as mentioned earlier, the abduction of Brazilian farmer Antonio Villas Boas had not yet been made public. This meant that the Hills would not have heard of that case or been able to base their story on it.

The two incidents are extremely similar, but were reported completely independently of each other in different countries.

The second important piece of evidence that backs up the Hill's story comes, strangely enough, from the military. After the Hills made their report, it was revealed that nearby Pease Air Force base had tracked a UFO that night on radar. The unknown object's appearance and departure matched the timing of the Hill's sighting.

This radar track provides impressive third person evidence that something very strange really did happen to the Hills during their drive home.

File No: 6499-03
Dateline: 5 November, 1975
Location: Snowflake, Arizona, USA

At the end of a hard day's work, seven members of a wood-cutting gang drove through the forest heading for home. On the journey back they drove over the top of a small hill and were stunned to find a disc-shaped UFO. The object gave out a gold glow and was witnessed by all seven men in the truck.

One of the workers, Travis Walton, ran towards the UFO. His friends watched in horror as the craft seemed to fire a blue ray at Travis and he was knocked back. The driver of the truck sped away from the site leaving Travis alone with the craft.

A short time later, the six remaining men gathered their courage and returned to the area, but there was no sign of either the craft or Travis. He had vanished.

SUSPECTED OF MURDER

The men reported what they had seen to the local police and found themselves in a lot of trouble.

As time dragged on and Travis stayed missing, the police began to suspect that the six men had murdered their colleague. They thought that the UFO report was just a cover story to hide the crime. [Although if this had been the case, it would surely be the weakest alibi in the history of crime.]

At one point, the police even asked the men to take a lie detector test. They passed.

Travis stayed missing for five days until he reappeared on 10 November in a confused and dazed state. He said that he had been abducted by short grey aliens who he described as having large heads and big black eyes.

While Travis was missing the media had become very interested in the mystery of his whereabouts. Suspecting a hoax, they also asked him to take a lie detector test to back up his incredible story. He took the test and he too passed.

'In the two decades since this multi-witness abduction first became news,' says Lorne Mason, 'not one of the original seven men has broken ranks and admitted making up the tale. They all stick by their story as the truth even today.'

File No: 6745-33
Dateline: 27 January, 1977
Location: Prospect, Kentucky, USA

Driving home in his jeep, Lee Parrish remembered seeing a UFO silently flying above his vehicle for a few minutes.

Once home he realised that the seven minute drive from his girlfriend's house had actually taken him forty five minutes. His mother called a local UFO group and they arranged for Lee to undergo a session of hypnotic regression.

LIVING RECTANGLE SLABS

Under the influence, Lee remembered blacking out as the UFO hovered over his jeep. The next thing he recalled was being in a white room surrounded by three of the most bizarre aliens ever reported.

Lee found himself being examined by a huge black slab that was almost as tall as the room itself. The slab had an articulated rod-like arm and Lee felt very strongly that the slab was alive and conscious.

Also in the room near Lee was a white rectangular object about the size of a drinks vending machine and Lee somehow got the impression that this one was the leader of the three. Finally there was a smaller red object that also had an arm-like device attached to it.

The black and red slabs touched Lee, causing him a small amount of pain. He felt that they were studying his chemical composition and later likened the experience to being a rat in a lab experiment. After this, the beings seemed to move towards each other and merge. Then they disappeared and moments later, Lee was back driving his jeep.

The local investigators who talked to Lee at the time were sure that he was telling the truth – at least as he saw it. Lorne Mason describes Lee's report as 'probably the weirdest alien encounter ever'.

File No: 6822-01
Dateline: 29 November, 1980
Location: Todmorden, Yorkshire, England

A disproportionate number of abduction reports seem to come from the USA and this might be because hypnosis is used as a memory-jogger more frequently in the USA than it is elsewhere. However, there have been many abduction incidents in the UK and other countries.

Northern England has been the setting for two reports of particular interest.

A POLICEMAN'S REPORT

Policeman PC Alan Godfrey was abducted from his police car when he was heading back towards Todmorden police station.

As Godfrey drove along he spotted the UFO hovering over the road ahead of him. At first he thought that a bus had turned over, but getting closer he saw a diamond-shaped craft hovering about two metres above the ground.

INTRODUCTION TO AN ALIEN

Under hypnotic regression later, the policeman recalled being taken inboard the UFO. A tall man with a beard introduced himself as 'Joseph'. This is very unusual because alien abductors don't usually like to give their names, even Earthly ones. [Probably because they're worried about complaints.]

Godfrey also remembered seeing other much stranger creatures lurking in the background as he was examined.

After his regression, Alan Godfrey did not know what to make of his new 'memories' and remained open-minded about the incident. It is worth adding that several other police patrols did report seeing strange lights over the area that very same night.

Seven years later, another case from the north of England would provide photographic evidence of its reality.

File No: 8499-06
Dateline: 1 December, 1987
Location: Ilkley Moor, Yorkshire, England

Early one crisp December morning, Philip Spencer set out across Ilkley moor in Yorkshire to visit a relative's house. Passing near a hilltop quarry, Spencer was surprised as he spotted a short green creature ahead of him.

The creature was about one and a third metres tall with big black eyes and pointed ears. Its long arms ended in huge hands with three fingers. The creature disappeared around an outcrop of rock. Spencer followed it and found himself confronted by a sleek silver disc. Before he could react, the craft rose quickly and disappeared into the sky.

ALIENS ON FILM

During this encounter, Spencer had managed to take a colour photograph of the being with his camera. Immediately afterwards he took the film into town to have it developed, unsure if he had captured the creature on film or not.

When the prints came back, it was there. The shot was blurred and grainy, but clearly showed the outline of the little green being. The negative of the 'alien shot' were later examined by experts at Kodak who said that the film had not been interfered with in any way.

Spencer was surprised to find that during the incident two hours had passed without him having any recollection of it. He under went a hypnotic regression to try and fill in the missing details.

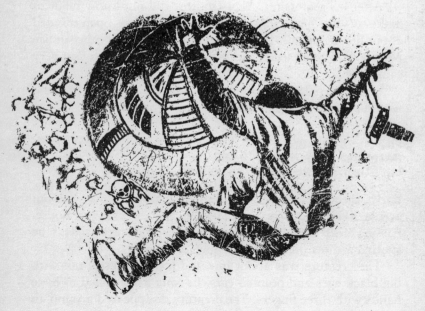

In the regression he recalled that after he had first seen the craft he was suspended in mid-air and floated inside it by the creature. Spencer was placed on a table in a white room and three of the creatures examined him using some kind of scanning device.

A WARNING FOR THE WORLD

After a break, Spencer was escorted to another room in the ship where he watched a series of film-like images relating to pollution and the damage that humankind is doing to the planet Earth. As we will see again later, warnings of ecological disaster are a common theme in many abduction accounts.

The next thing Spencer remembered was being back on the moor and taking the photograph of the entity before watching the ship leave.

The man involved in this case has always asked that his name be kept out of the publicity and so the pseudonym Philip Spencer is usually used by UFOlogists instead. Spencer always refused to try and make any money out of his alien photo, and even went as far as assigning its copyright to an UFO investigator because he wanted to make sure that the incident was looked into as thoroughly as possible.

As well as Spencer's eyewitness account and the photograph he took, there is one more piece of evidence for this case. Lorne Mason reports: 'After the event Spencer found that the polarity of a pocket compass he was carrying had been reversed. It now pointed towards south instead of north.'

THE NEW WAVE

Recently claims of alien abduction have grabbed the headlines and magazine covers all over the world. In America particularly, there have been a crop of new abduction reports. This latest wave seemed to follow the publication of Whitley Strieber's book Communion.

File No: WS-9349 - The Strieber Files
Dateline: 1985-on
Location: America

Starting in the winter of 1985, the American novelist Whitley Strieber became involved in a series of abduction events involving aliens he dubbed 'the Visitors'. These beings seemed to be a variation of the traditional Grey. Strieber claimed to have had repeated visits from these entities at his country cabin.

The story of his contacts and his struggle to believe and cope with the experience became a very successful book titled Communion which stayed on the New York Times best-seller list for months, generating a huge amount of publicity and new interest in abductions.

In the years that followed, Strieber and UFOlogists received a surge of abduction reports with a large proportion of them (but by no means all) featuring aliens as portrayed in the book.

Sceptics and UFO debunkers were quick to seize on this as proof that the claims were copycat fantasies. Strieber and his supporters argued that the visitors are real and therefore the new reports were similar to his because they are based on the same experience.

Whichever is the case it is certainly true that the number of abduction claims and people's interest in them continues to rise.

CHAPTER 4
The Chosen

As we have seen, during the last few decades a huge variety of UFOs and their alien occupants have been reported by bewildered witnesses.

In the next four chapters we will take a detailed look at a number of specially selected cases and the issues that they raise for UFOlogists, the people who try to understand them. Later on we will consider the arguments against abductions taking place at all, but for the moment, let us assume that they are real events.

The incidents that we have covered so far give the immediate impression of being random occurrences. The aliens appear to be out looking for someone ... anyone, and a person on a lonely road late at night finds that they are the unfortunate 'victim' in the wrong place at the wrong time.

A MORE SINISTER PLAN

In many cases this does seem to be what happens, but American investigator Budd Hopkins has potentially uncovered another much more sinister system.

Hopkins has investigated over one thousand cases and believes that some abductees are taken and examined on many repeated occasions. He has evidence from witnesses that the aliens have a programme or game plan for who they abduct. One individual may be 'picked up' on a number of occasions over a period of decades.

The ideas that Budd Hopkins puts forward are obviously controversial. Some other investigators find them 'too wild' to swallow, but Hopkins has a good reputation, especially for witness care. His cases are well documented and as we shall see they include some impressive physical evidence as well as abductee reports.

The strange experience of subject Kathie Davis has been described as a 'state of the art' American abduction case.

C/S File No: 9458-34
Name: Kathie Davis (aka Debbie Tomey)
Dateline: 1966 to present
Location: Indiana, USA

THEY KEEP COMING BACK

Kathie Davis was born in 1959 in Indiana, USA. She is the divorced mother of two small boys and at the time of one of her major abduction incidents she was living back at home with her parents.

She first got in touch with Budd Hopkins in 1983 after reading his book Missing Time, which told the stories of

seven alien abductions. Kathie had written to Hopkins because she felt that she too might have had a similar experience.

Her letter sparked a long investigation, the results of which were presented to the public in another book entitled Intruders. Under hypnosis Kathie seemed to reveal a history of repeated abductions of both herself and other family members.

Kathie claimed that her first encounter took place in the winter of 1966 when she was six years old. She was playing outside at a friend's house in Detroit when there was a flash of light and a loud noise.

Kathie then found herself in a white, windowless room and saw a small figure who first appeared to be a 'little boy'. However later, 'he' changed into a small grey-coloured alien with a large head. The creature had a machine that then made some kind of cut in her lower leg, a scar that she still has today. After this procedure she was returned to an area near the house.

SERIAL ABDUCTION

The next series of abduction incidents were scattered through her late teen years. Aged sixteen, Kathie saw four spiralling lights in the sky and odd humanoid figures below them in a local park.

Two years later, Kathie and two friends were out driving late at night in the countryside when they spotted a UFO in the night sky. The craft landed and Kathie was taken on board and medically examined by the same small grey-faced figure that she had reported seeing before at the age of six. Again in March 1978 and in the summer of 1979, Kathie remembers an abduction experience and a subsequent examination by grey figures.

On 30 June, 1983 a major incident occurred for which there was not only Kathie's first hand testimony, but an independent witness and some hard physical evidence. It was this event which had made Kathie write to Budd Hopkins in the first place.

WHITE LIGHTS

The 30 June was a hot and humid summer's day. At about nine o'clock in the evening, Kathie spotted a 'funny-coloured light glowing from inside' the family pool house in the garden. When Kathie went to investigate it later on her way out to a friend's house, she found that it was gone.

A short time afterwards Kathie's mother saw 'a pale white light' surrounding the bird feeder in the garden. She rang Kathie who returned home to check the house for intruders. A nervous Kathie searched the house and back yard, carrying an unloaded shotgun for added security, but found nothing. While stalking around the back yard with the unloaded gun, Kathie's dog, Penny, seemed unsettled and scared. She then went back to her friend's house, but when she arrived Kathie realised that she had lost an hour of time somewhere along the line.

Months later, using hypnotic regression, Kathie and Budd Hopkins tried to uncover what had happened in that missing time.

Kathie now recalled coming across an egg-shaped craft on four jointed landing legs that was sitting in the middle of the grass. A ball of bright white light approached Kathie and moved up and down the length of her body as if scanning her in some way. A familiar feature of many cases.

WHISPERING

Then came the most frightening part of the whole experience. She saw 'six dark things' outlined against the light. She described them as being roughly her height, smooth and without any features, 'kind of shaped like big bullets'.

The creatures came towards her and one whispered her name 'Kathie!'. At around this point a medical probe of some sort was inserted into her ear causing her more than a little discomfort. The experience ended with another burst of bright light, presumably as the craft left and headed into the sky.

With just Kathie's reports of her own abduction experiences as evidence, even the most open-minded person might have trouble believing them. The encounters might even seem rather self-centred. Why should aliens be so very interested in one person as to keep coming back to her? However, for this particular experience of 30 June, 1983 Hopkins also provides two strong pieces of independent evidence.

ALL SHOOK UP

The Davis family's nearest neighbour, Joyce Lloyd, was at home on the evening of the alleged abduction. She remembers being in her dining room when there was a sudden flash of light from the direction of the Davis' backyard.

Joyce then felt her house start to vibrate as if a jet plane was passing very close overhead. As she described it, 'The house shook like it felt as if the entire yard was shaking.' The lights in the dining room flickered and the picture on the TV turned completely red in colour. Then just as suddenly, the noise stopped and everything returned to normal.

Although Joyce Lloyd did not claim to have seen anything like the UFO itself, her report is hard to explain away. [Kathie would have needed a pretty powerful imagination to make up her bizarre tales in the first place; she would need a very powerful imagination indeed to vibrate Mrs Lloyd's dining-room.]

INCREDIBLE HEAT

One of the factors that make it hard for many sceptics and scientists to take abduction reports seriously is the lack of physical evidence. How can so many UFOs move around without leaving some solid traces behind them? In this case the UFO may have done just that.

Kathie found that there was a circle of burned grass and soil where she had seen the craft land. This area was still 'warm to the touch' nearly an hour later. Hopkins organised for soils samples to be taken both from the affected burnt area and from another part of the back yard.

To duplicate the soil colour of the burnt sample, the normal soil had to be heated to 600°F (approximately 315°C) for six hours. Clearly, whatever had caused this circle was something capable of unleashing huge amounts of energy or heat.

Nothing would grow on the burnt area for over two years after the incident and the markings remained clearly visible in the family's backyard as an unwelcome reminder of that night's events.

A WARNING

When investigator Budd Hopkins first started researching Kathie's case he warned her that the abductions would most probably stop when she started to be investigated. This was normally the way things happened, but not this time.

Kathie continued to have abduction episodes even while the earlier ones were being documented. Kathie's experiences were published in Budd Hopkins' book, Intruders.

Since then the experiencer has dropped her Kathie Davis pseudonym and 'gone public' under her real name of Debbie Tomey, although in most UFO books she is often still referred to as Kathie Davis.

STAKE OUT

Abduction expert Lorne Mason has followed Kathie Davis' case with interest: 'I've read through many of the transcripts of Kathie's hypnotic regression sessions and they seem to be an honest and very emotional account of events. Kathie really does seem to believe that they happened to her. However we know that under hypnosis the subconscious mind is capable of making past events up to create a 'fantasy reality'. Although the burn marks are good physical evidence which back up Kathie's account, even they are not conclusive.'

Like most observers, Mason would like more concrete proof: 'Cases like this one are both promising and frustrating for investigators. If the aliens do keep returning, perhaps Hopkins and his team could install cameras or tape recorders in Kathie's home and try to capture the most convincing evidence of all – the abduction event on film.'

WHY ME?

What is the purpose of these abductions? Why does someone or something have such an interest in Kathie?

The answer that she and Budd Hopkins put forward is the most bizarre and wildest piece of the whole puzzle.

They claim that the ultimate purpose of Kathie's abductions is to allow the grey-skinned aliens to develop a human-alien hybrid baby. Their plan is to create a new species that is somehow a genetic combination of humans and aliens.

This hybrid-breeding idea occurs in many, many abduction reports. Among others it was present in the case of Brazilian, Antonio Villas Boas (see Chapter 2 File No: 4129–33 page 22). The young farmer was introduced to a human looking woman during his abduction as far back as 1957.

Abductees such as Linda Cortile (see Chapter 1, File No: 9732–04 page 8) have also recounted the aliens' desire to interbreed with humankind. Looking back through the case histories on record, we can see that this theme crops up in a very large number of abductions. Abductees are sometimes shown babies or are even given babies to hold and cradle for a short time.

MORE QUESTIONS THAN ANSWERS

Why are they doing this? All aliens are notoriously tight-lipped about themselves and their motives. On the rare occasion when a frightened abductee does ask a question, it is usually ignored. The obvious answer though, and one very occasionally given by the aliens, is that they, as a species, are unable to breed.

The aliens' scheme to create hybrid babies is now well documented in many books and articles, but what is important is that such details were reported by many other abductees independently of each other before they were made public.

In the 1970s, a young woman from the north of England reported a scenario remarkable similar to that of Kathie Davis. Her little known case was on file with British UFOlogist Jenny Randles long before Hopkins published his work, so the woman could not have copied or drawn on any details from that.

For many reasons this is the most bizarre and also the most disturbing aspect of aliens abductions.

Do the aliens have a long term plan beyond just observing humankind? Do their medical examinations have a purpose above and beyond idle curiosity? Many abductees say that they do. Most scientists and sceptics dismiss such ideas as paranoid fantasies, but they may turn out to be the biggest mystery in the whole alien enigma.

ALIEN IMPLANTS

Just as interesting are the claims made by abductees that the alien beings have put some kind of implant into their bodies. Budd Hopkins believes that this may be the answer to the puzzle of how the aliens are able to locate a certain person to re-abduct them. He believes that implants may have been used over the years of Kathie Davis' abductions.

According to many abductees, a small device is put under their skin during a short surgical procedure on board the craft. No one has yet come up with an explanation for why the aliens would want to do this, except to use it as some kind of tracking signal.

Although implants are a much discussed issue among UFOlogists, most experts are sceptical as to their existence. For all the talk about them, no one has yet recovered an implant from an abductee and proved it to be of extraterrestrial origin. Indeed, finding a working alien implant in an abductee has almost become the 'Holy Grail' of UFOlogy for some investigators.

THE SEARCH FOR PROOF

If such an object was to be discovered and proven to be made from non-Earthly materials then it would truly be evidence that would confirm the reality of alien visitors. The only trouble is that the results of 'implants' so far recovered have been disappointing.

A long term abductee had what he claimed was a implant removed from his leg by a human doctor after it had been in place for 34 years. When it was analyzed later using a scanning electron microscope, the implant first appeared to be a 'shard of glass'.

On closer inspection the microscope revealed what was described as 'a strange surface structure' and the specialist went as far as to pronounce it as a 'mineral anomaly', but that was far from the proof of alien technology that the investigators were hoping for.

It seems unlikely at this time that any such proof will be forthcoming from the field of implant investigations. Even if they did exit, surely the aliens are too cunning and too clever to ever allow UFOlogists to prove their existence by removing a tell-tale device they had left themselves.

Whether they are real or not, implants are certainly a fascinating idea and the theme has been taken up and used in X-Files stories like the pilot episode – where alien implants are recovered from a group of teenagers – and the 'Duane Barry'/'Ascension' two-parter where Agent Scully herself is 'abducted'.

Chris Carter, the man who created The X-Files, has said that it was partly the work of people like Budd Hopkins and John Mack that inspired him to make the series in the first place. Although The X-Files draws much of its inspiration from UFO events like the weird case of Kathie Davis, for the real Kathie there is no turning off the television at the end of an episode and walking away. For Kathie, everyday life is an ongoing X-File.

CHAPTER 5
Messages of Disaster

When comparing abduction reports from around the world there are some very obvious themes that reoccur time and time again. One of these is the idea of hybrid alien-human babies as we have seen in the case of Kathie Davis. Another very commonly reported event is the eco-warning or lecture. Having been spacenapped and then examined by the entities, the abductee is given a dire warning about the future of the entire planet.

When comparing accounts of the warnings handed out, it quickly becomes clear that the aliens have a very low opinion of how humankind is treating the planet Earth.

In recent abductions the vast majority of the warnings seem to be about the ecological damage that humankind is doing to the world. Before this however, the warnings tended to be about the dangers of the atomic bomb and the threat of nuclear war. In California, two friends were given just such a warning by what they claimed were two aliens who looked like giant brains.

C/S File No: 5395-04
Name: John Hodges and Peter Rodriguez
Dateline: August 1971
Location: Dapple Grey Lane, California, USA

John Hodges and Peter Rodriguez were driving through south Los Angeles at two in the morning. They were returning to their homes from a friend's house when their attention was distracted by a beam of white light coming from some trees near the road side.

GIANT FLOATING BRAINS

Using their car headlights to illuminate the area, they were amazed to see two creatures resembling large human brains in front of them. The larger brain was about one metre high and had a bright red spot near the top of it. The smaller brain (which was only seen by Hodges) was about the size of a football.

The wrinkled but seemingly intelligent entities floated near the car window screen observing the men. The startled men gathered their senses and drove away into the night as fast as they could. Hodges got back to his home at 4:30 a.m., two hours later than he should have – a classic episode of missing time.

Under hypnotic regression, Hodges recalled sitting in his car and asking the strange brains why they had come to him instead of someone else. He then found himself transported to a white room where he saw very tall grey humanoid figures. The humanoid figures seemed to be in charge and told Hodges that the two brains were only there to act as translators.

NUCLEAR EXPLOSIONS

The larger brain told Hodges that the aliens had been watching this world with concern because it had too much destructive power in the form of atomic bombs. Hodges was shown a giant image of the Earth displayed on what he described as 'a super advanced hologram'.

Across the surface of the globe, various locations were highlighted areas where the aliens said that the danger of destruction was the greatest. Hodges was then shown a series of atomic explosions taking place at the North and South Poles of the planet. [Although of course the North Pole is an unlikely target in a nuclear war unless you're trying to bomb Santa Claus.]

The picture changed and Hodges found himself viewing images of a barren wasteland on a 'dead' planet. The atmosphere was unbreathable and the pollution was so bad that every living thing had been wiped out. Images like these are a common feature of alien eco-lectures to witnesses.

Sometimes the aliens seem to be showing witnesses an image because it is what could happen to the Earth if humankind does not change its ways. On other occasions they claim that this is what has already happened on their home world, and they want to make sure that humans do not repeat their mistakes.

GETTING IT WRONG

The beings then made some predictions, among other things telling Hodges that there would be a world-wide nuclear war in the mid-eighties. [In case you haven't seen the news in the last decade – there wasn't.]

Hodges was returned to his car and the entities told him that they would meet again at some point in the future.

In time that prediction (and others) turned out to be hopelessly wrong and Hodges decided that he could not trust the strange beings. However he remained convinced that his meeting with them really did happen.

C/S File No: 8971-22
Name: Ed
Dateline: July 1961
Location: Maine, USA

Many people find themselves changed by their experiences as abductees. One such individual is Ed, a man now in his mid-forties.

Ed's abduction encounter is one of many to be investigated by the Pulitzer Prize-winning John Mack. Ed's abduction happened in July of 1961, but he did not recall it in anything like full detail until over three decades later. Ed was referred to Professor John Mack who used hypnotic regression to explore the incident beyond Ed's conscious memories.

AN ALIEN VACATION

Ed's case is an interesting story and provides us with a very good example of alien ecological warnings. It also had a great impact on Ed's life afterwards.

The incident occurred when Ed was on vacation with a friend, Bob, and Bob's parents. The group was touring up the coast of Maine and had stopped at a place near Portland. Bob's parents rented a cabin for the night and the two boys slept in the back of the family car which was parked about one hundred metres from the sea.

CREATURES IN THE FOG

A thick sea fog drifted in towards them from the crashing surf. Ed began to feel a little frightened, but tried to get off to sleep. He awoke a short time later and was alarmed to see figures moving around near the car. He had to struggle to see them through the fog but described them as not looking like normal humans. 'They had big black eyes and intense small mouths.'

Ed felt a tingling at the back of his neck and felt himself floating out of the car and travelling over the breaking waves of the ocean. His destination was a 'luminescent, dome-like pod' and he remembered being floated inside through its underside.

In the craft, Ed found himself surrounded by 'at least six beings' in a room lit by white light. A female humanoid seemed to have the role of head doctor and she examined him and took medical samples.

A LECTURE FROM SPACE

The next thing Ed remembered was being in a different room on the craft. The female entity reappeared and somehow Ed knew that she had 'important things' to tell him.

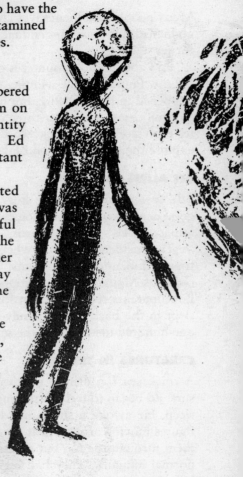

The being communicated with Ed telepathically as he was shown a series of powerful images of destruction of the Earth, and she expressed her grave concerns about the way humankind were treating the planet.

Ed recalled seeing: 'the Earth shuddering in anguish, crying and weeping at the stupidity of humans'. The alien kept explaining to Ed that 'the laws of the universe are this way, and if you keep driving on the wrong side of the road then look what's going to happen'.

Ed was told that the Earth's skin was going to swat humankind off as if they were bugs. Naturally Ed asked what he could do prevent this taking place, but was told nothing could stop it. 'Too few will listen.'

CHANGING LIVES

After Ed had recalled this strange and worrying encounter he felt that he really did want to stop man damaging the planet. Like many abductees the powerful emotions that they felt during the experience lived with him afterwards and he has taken a far more active stand to do whatever he can to help.

Ed is far from being the only person whose values have been changed or challenged by an abduction experience. Investigators have found a familiar pattern which they can sometimes use to help confirm a suspected abduction.

File No: 6529-77
Dateline: 27 October, 1974
Location: Aveley, Essex, England

The family involved in the 'Aveley Abduction' (see Chapter 1, File No: 6529–77 page 7) also underwent important changes after their night-time experience.

John and Sue Avis and three children were driving home through the autumn countryside late at night when Kevin (the oldest son) noticed an oval-shaped light in the sky. The electric-blue light seemed to be keeping pace with their car and they watched it with interest as they drove along the quiet country lane.

INTO THE FOG

Eventually the light disappeared from sight behind some trees and the family thought that they had seen the last of it. The 'light', however, had very different ideas.

About a mile further down the road the Avis car turned a corner and the family saw a bank of thick luminous green fog covering the road ahead of them. As the car drove into the fog, its engine went dead and the vehicle shuddered violently.

The next thing the family remembered was driving out of the glowing fog and completing the journey home. When they arrived back at their house, it was three hours later than it should have been.

After that night, the five family members begun having strange and frightening dreams and other almost 'poltergeist'-like activity took place in the house. Having chanced upon an article in the local press about UFOs, John sought help. Investigator and author Andrew Collins researched their case and used hypnosis to uncover the experience further. It was the first time that hypnosis had ever been used in a British abduction investigation.

ON BOARD THE CRAFT

Under hypnosis John recalled finding himself inside what looked like an alien craft gazing out over a large hanger area. John's wife Sue was next to him, and behind them was a tall figure who was one of the craft's occupants. During his hypnosis, John referred to these tall entities as 'the Watchers'.

John was taken into what he described as 'an examination room' where he was looked over by two repulsive hairy creatures wearing white coats like doctors. Three of the taller entities who wore silver one piece outfits stood behind them observing the proceedings.

After the medical, John was taken on a tour of the ship and had its two propulsion systems explained to him. [If you're interested in building a spacecraft – they were an 'ion drive' for use in deep space and a magnetic system for use inside planetary atmospheres.]

THE END OF THE WORLD

The tour ended in a kind of control room and John laid back and watched a disc-shaped screen as it began to show him images.

He saw a holographic picture of a number of dull grey cone-shaped buildings sitting under an inflamed sky. John was told that this sorry scene was the result of pollution on Earth. The show ended. John was taken and 'put' back in his car

with the rest of his family and returned to their lonely Essex road.

The incident had a long term effect on the family and they made some serious and permanent changes to their life-styles afterwards. Four members of the family gave up eating meat and found that they were much more comfortable living as vegetarians, (a life-style much less common in the 1970s than today). John, who was formally a heavy smoker, gave up smoking completely and the couple became much more active in environmental and spiritual matters than they ever had been before.

A SIGN OF THE TIMES

Other abductees have reported going through similar transformations. In general, abductees tend to feel more interested in and connected with the natural world around them.

UFO debunkers are right to point out that the warnings given by the aliens have changed over the years. In the early days the aliens were full of gloom and doom about the atomic bomb, but as time went on, their warnings started to concentrate the ecological plight of the Earth.

Sceptics would say that the concerns of the aliens mirror our own human worries just a little too closely for comfort. Perhaps somehow abductees project their own fears for the future into their experiences? UFOlogists, however, would argue that aliens have been giving us ecology lessons a long time before the subject became fashionable or front page news.

CHAPTER 6

The Little People

Alien abductions are usually thought of as a modern phenomenon, but stories about humans being stolen away by strange entities can be traced back over many centuries.

The tales take the form of fairy stories and they include many elements that would sound remarkably familiar to UFOlogists. Some of whom have researched into fairy myths in an attempt to get a better understanding of the abduction enigma.

SMALL SILVER PEOPLE

Many fairy stories tell of humans going about their normal business and encountering strange small people, often green or silver in colour. Until last century these ancient stories would have been handed down by word of mouth from one generation to the next. Today such folklore has been relegated to historical trivia, which is a great shame because many people in the past believed that they described real events.

Sometimes the meeting (or encounter as we would say today) begins with the arrival of eerie 'fairy lights' floating in the air. On other occasions people chance upon 'fairy rings', – circular patterns on the ground which have more than a passing resemblance to the landing marks left by modern day UFOs. In Ireland, one of the Celtic strongholds, it was a common belief that fairies travelled through the sky in 'spectre ships' and the origin of the little folk was specifically remembered as being 'another planet'.

STOLEN AWAY

According to Celtic folklore these 'little people' (also known as 'the hidden people') could bewitch or charm normal folk into following them back to the fairy realm. Once they had entered the 'otherworld' they would see fantastic sights, and life afterwards was never quite the same again.

Upon their return to human society the person was often surprised to find that they had been away for much longer than they had realised. Although the experience seemed to last a few minutes they had actually been away for hours, days or sometimes even years. People used to say that 'time passes differently with the wee folk', just as it seems to during UFO events.

MISSING FOR TWO YEARS

An old folklore tale collected by writer Edwin Hartland describes how a young boy disappears from his village and remains missing for two years. One day there is a knock on the mother's door and it is the boy still wearing exactly the same clothes as when he vanished and not a day older.

His mother asks where he has been all this time and he replies that he was with the 'little people, but it was only yesterday that I went away'. The boy then shows her an item of clothing he has been given which is 'made of paper without a seam'.

The one piece lightweight outfit in the story sounds alarmingly like the clothes usually reported to be worn by UFO occupants. Other fairy stories contain ever stranger parallels to alien abductions.

STAR-WORSHIPPERS

In the traditional Cornish story 'The Fairy Dwelling on Selena Moor', Mr Noy – a local farmer – sets out walking one night and goes missing for three days. When the unconscious Mr Noy is found by his worried friends he is convinced that he has only been away a short time.

Mr Noy describes what happened to him. He was taking a short cut across the moor (which he knew very well) and had somehow got himself lost. He wandered around until he spotted some lights in the distance and headed towards them in the hope that it would be a friendly house.

His dog refused to go any nearer and backed away as Mr Noy approached what he now saw was a gathering of 'very small' people sitting at tables eating and drinking. To his surprise and delight, Mr Noy met his sweetheart who everyone believed to be dead.

The young woman described the fairies as 'star-worshippers' and said curiously 'They have little sense or feeling ... what serves them best is whatever pleased them when they lived as mortals thousands of years ago.'

Mr Noy tried to rescue the girl from the fairies' power, but was knocked unconscious and remembered nothing until he was found by the search party of villagers.

TOO CLOSE FOR COMFORT?

Within this one short narrative there is:

1) A night time encounter with a strange light.
2) Small humanoid beings that are somehow connected to the stars.
3) A frightened reaction of a dog.
4) The idea that the beings have 'little sense or feeling': a phrase that well describes how Greys examine their abductees.
5) A period of missing time.

All of these elements would fit perfectly into an abduction report, but this story was recorded by writer W. Bottrell as early as 1870 and is probably much older than that.

CHANGELINGS

Numerous fairy myths also include the fairies' desire to steal human children and babies, sometimes putting a 'changeling' in the human infant's place. Fairies are also famous for wanting to interbreed with humans to 'reinforce their fairy stock'. This theme is uncannily close to the idea of hybrid babies that some witnesses claim to see on board alien ships.

The following case illustrates the kind of strange and nonsensical behaviour that appears in fairy myths, along with an exchange of food that is also a regular feature of such stories. However, it is not another fairy story from the past – this is a contemporary UFO report.

C/S File No: 4883-03
Dateline: 18 April, 1961
Location: Eagle River, Wisconsin, USA

Joe Simonton lived alone in a house near Eagle River in Wisconsin. At eleven o'clock one morning he was disturbed by a loud rumbling noise coming from outside his house. He stepped outside to investigate and saw a shining saucer-like craft hovering in his back yard. It was 'brighter than chrome' and measured about ten metres across by four metres tall.

A doorway opened and Simonton could see three figures moving around inside. Simonton described them as

'resembling Italians': having olive skin, dark hair, and wearing black two piece outfits.

One of the figures came forward holding a jug that appeared to be made of the same material as the ship. The figure gestured to the empty jug indicating to Simonton that he needed some water, and the sixty-year-old farmer hospitably took the jug into his house and returned with it full.

SPACE FOOD

As Simonton handed over the water, he saw that the figures inside the ship were cooking food on some kind of flameless grill. The ship's interior seemed to be mostly black in colour, although Simonton did catch sight of what looked like computer control panels.

Simonton showed an interest in what was being prepared and one of the figures gave him a sample – three small biscuit-like pancakes, each about eight cm across.

The craft stayed in Simonton's back yard for a total of about five minutes. One of the figures then closed the hatch and the ship took off, heading in a southerly direction at great speed and bending local trees out of shape as it passed over them.

JUST BIZARRE

On the face of it this is a nonsensical story and it is that which links it so strongly with age-old fairy tales. It is completely unbelievable that aliens capable of travelling through space would need to stop to borrow a jug of water to make pancakes.

The old farmer insisted that the United States Department of Health Education and Welfare analyse the pancakes.

They performed chemical, infra-red and radiation tests but found them to be quite unexceptional. The ingredients were all of everyday origin. The only interesting feature was that they were totally lacking in salt. This again ties the case into fairy lore because fairy folk are well known in legend to never eat salt.

A CLOSE ENCOUNTER OF THE ABSURD KIND

Simonton bravely ate one of the extraterrestrial snacks but nothing weird or interesting happened as a result. 'It tasted like cardboard', was his rather disappointed verdict.

As a witness, Simonton was described as sincere and obviously believed what he was telling people. Why would he have invented such a silly story? He gained nothing from reporting it to the authorities, except perhaps strange looks from his neighbours.

Many other alien encounters are just as bizarre. Author Whitley Strieber quotes odd events in reports that he has received from his readers.

One correspondent explained: 'You are not going to believe this, but they came out of the cooking stove.' Other people have been surprised to find alien beings stepping out of their bedroom wardrobes in the middle of the night.

A METHOD IN THEIR MADNESS?

Many scientists and sceptics find it hard to take aliens abductions and UFOs seriously precisely because of the aliens' odd behaviour.

Surely, the scientists reason, aliens would be more intelligent, more evolved and more logical than the way witnesses report them behaving. Of course, here scientists are entirely coloured by their own views as to what is 'sensible behaviour'. There may be a method in the aliens madness that we do not understand.

Looking closely at the reports of witnesses suggests, however, that nonsensical actions and just plain weirdness are absolutely central to the entire UFO and abduction event just as they have been in fairy lore for centuries. Certainly such behaviour is right at the heart of fairy myths, where trickery and mischief often seem to be the fairy peoples' main aim.

C/S FILE NO: 67840-54
DATELINE: 4 January, 1979
Location: Rowley Regis, Birmingham, England

The most fairy-like of all alien encounters occurred on a cold January morning in England and became for ever immortalised in the national press as the 'Mince Pie Martians'.

Jean Hingley was seeing her husband off to work early one morning when she noticed an orange light in the garden. At first she thought that her husband, Cyril, had left a light on somewhere, but as she got closer she saw that the light was coming from an orange sphere hanging over the garden. The lights came closer and turned white illuminating the entire garden. Mrs Hingley could feel the heat that the sphere was generating on her face.

WINGS LIKE PAPER

Without warning, three beings floated past Mrs Hingley making a buzzing noise as they headed inside her house through the back door.

The entities were just over one metre tall and had beautiful rainbow-coloured wings on their back. The wings looked delicate as if they were made of thin paper. The three little men were dressed in a silver-green colour and had helmets over their heads. Their body size and facial features (big black eyes) sound very similar to the Greys, except of course that these beings had wings.

Mrs Hingley's dog collapsed to the floor in a deep sleep and Mrs Hingley felt herself being floated into the living-room. Inside, the three entities were floating around touching as many of the everyday objects in the room as they could. They showed particular interest in the Christmas tree which was still standing and gave it a good shake.

MAGNETIC HANDS

In what was over an hour long encounter, Mrs Hingley nervously engaged them in conversation. The beings

63

complained that they had come down from the sky 'to try and talk to people, but they don't seem to be interested'.

At one point, the three men landed on the family sofa and began jumping up and down on it. When Mrs Hingley asked them to stop, a thin laser beam came out of the top of one of their helmets and hurt her eyes.

The being's arms ended in simple points rather than hands and they seemed to pick things up using magnetic properties. They handled several cassette tapes that were in the room and the recordings on them were later found to have been ruined. Mrs Hingley's television, radio and her electric clock all suffered as well.

The stunned factory worker Mrs Hingley gave the visitors a mince pie each, which they gladly took, scooping them up with their seemingly magnetic 'points'.

A HASTY RETREAT

To steady her nerves, Mrs Hingley lit herself a cigarette which alarmed the beings. The frightened little men floated back outside to their orange craft and disappeared inside taking their mince pies with them. The craft flashed its exterior lights in what Mrs Hingley took to be a 'goodbye' and rose in the air flying away north.

The aliens' craft had left track marks in the thick snow where it had landed, and later as the snow melted the family realised they extended down into the soil below.

After they had gone, Mrs Hingley collapsed on to the floor and it was a while before she was strong enough to even telephone her husband for help. Her eyes received medical treatment and remained sore for weeks. [The dog made a speedier recovery.]

Here we have a case that combines technology such as laser beams and spacecraft with the secondary evidence of the ruined tapes and landing marks, as well as bizarre and fairy-like behaviour by the craft's occupants.

ALIENS BEHAVING BADLY

The strange beings claimed that no one on Earth would talk to them and responded with painful laser beams when asked to stop jumping up and down on a sofa. At first appearances, it is a ridiculous report. Surely anyone could make up a more believable alien encounter than that. But Jean Hingley sticks by her story as being exactly what happened.

FAIRIES OR ALIENS?

Many UFOlogists are much keener to document the more reasonable cases of contact where the aliens behave more 'sensibly' than the reports like Mrs Hingley's incident (usually known as the 'Rowley Regis case').

French UFO investigator Dr Jacques Vallee was one of the first people to study the similarities between UFO/abduction reports and stories from fairy folklore. He concluded that the two things may well be variations on a theme: different interpretations of just one phenomena that is adapted into the common language of the time. Many years ago people believed in fairies and elves; today they believe in flying saucers and aliens.

The parallels between modern abductions by 'aliens' and much older stories of people stolen away by 'fairies' are strong enough to be worthwhile looking at. However, to expect this alone to provide the answer to the abduction puzzle seems to be rather over-hopeful. It does not, for example, help us predict events or get closer to the phenomena itself.

ONE ANSWER?

Are fairy stories from folklore really recollections of encounters with aliens, or are today's grey-skinned abductors the modern incarnation of the mythical little people? The idea that fairies and UFOs are linked in some way is by no means impossible, but it seems to raise as many questions as it answers.

CHAPTER 7

Visitors From Beyond

If UFOs and their alien occupants really are visiting Earth, then where are they from? The answer, if you believe the aliens is just about everywhere. Witnesses have reported creatures claiming to originate from Sirius, Mars, Draco, Zeta Reticulii, and the Pleiades.

More often than not the startled human witness does not get the chance to ask any questions during the encounter. Even when they do, the aliens often seem incredibly vague about where they have come from saying things like 'we are from a distant galaxy' or 'our home is a larger planet than yours' or even more pointlessly, 'we are from the sky'. [Whether this is due to secrecy or a bad sense of direction remains to be seen.]

Witness sometimes get a feeling that the alien is just giving any old location as their home planet just to dismiss the question and avoid the truth.

POINTS OF ORIGIN

Even asking the question 'Where are they from?' assumes many things about the alien visitors, things that may not be true. Such a question takes for granted that the creatures are extraterrestrial and, more important still, it assumes that their home is in this universe.

Some investigators who have studied the phenomena believe that these 'extraterrestrial' life forms may in fact be 'extra-dimensional'. That is to say they maybe entering into our world from another dimension.

Many abductees feel that the aliens come from a place 'beyond the veil' as they describe it. Rather than flying into our atmosphere in nuts and bolts spaceships, many abductees feel or sense that the aliens are 'breaking in' to our world from somewhere else. A place one witness described as 'not very far away, but very different'.

Rather than beginning with a blast of wind from an flying saucer exhaust, most encounters begin with the silent arrival of a powerful blue or white light as if a doorway had suddenly been opened into a bright room.

CRACKS IN REALITY

Abductees rarely, if ever, see the aliens in the act of breaking or climbing in to their house. 'I saw a figure standing in the shadows who hadn't been there a moment before' and 'suddenly there were three of them by my bed' are typical comments. It is as if the creatures have slipped inside the room without actually needing to arrive.

A number of abductees interviewed by John Mack particularly reported that they thought their abductors took them out of this dimension. It is as if a tiny crack opens in our reality, and the visitors squeeze through it to enter our world.

UFOlogist Lorne Mason is particularly fascinated by this idea: 'Perhaps our alien visitors are not explorers from another star system. Perhaps they travel here from another dimension, stepping sideways into our own. What we take to be their spacecraft may be vehicles designed to travel between dimensions instead of between planets.'

Mason is not the first investigator to consider this as a serious possibility. In his best-selling book Dimensions, Dr Jacques Vallee says that he believes that the UFO phenomenon 'represents evidence for other dimensions beyond space-time'.

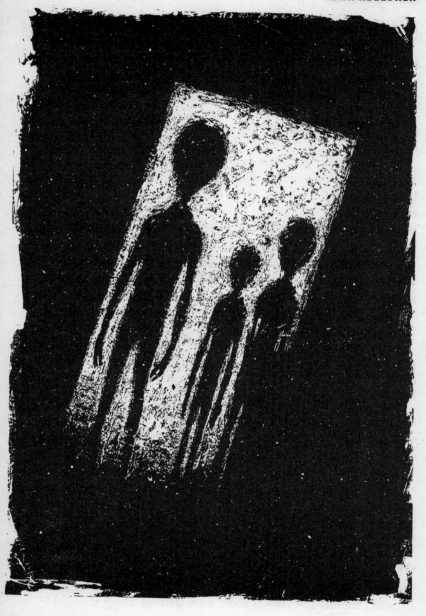

SHEER TERROR

If extraterrestrials are actually extra-dimensionals then this would explain much of the associated phenomena that goes with them. Their dimension may obey different physical laws to ours. A bridgehead between the two could easily cause the electrical and magnetic interference that is often seen during abductions.

It might also go some way to explaining the sheer and absolute terror that many abductees feel even when they have been treated relatively kindly by the visitors. Watching reality as you know it crumble in front of your eyes would be the most terrifying thing that could happen to any intelligent and aware lifeform.

Perhaps even their fantastical plans to breed hybrid babies are not designed to bring together species from two different planets, but from two separate realities. Maybe the aim is create a being that can survive in both dimensions or even travel between them both freely.

File No: WS-9349 - The Strieber Files
Dateline: 1985-on
Location: America

Communion author Whitley Strieber is also open to the idea that his visitors might be from another dimension. In his introduction to Vallee's book he says: 'The visitors are a dark and highly active phenomenon that seems to inhabit cracks in the unconscious, cracks in space-time, and cracks in history.'

As well as his regular contacts with the Visitors in our world Strieber has also had his own seemingly inter-dimensional journey.

OTHER WORLDS, OTHER PLACES

Strieber describes how one afternoon he was giving a lift to his son's friend. The two of them were driving along Route 17

in Strieber's
car heading
towards New York
when they reached
their exit on the
highway and turned off.

At this point, strange
things started to happen.
Instead of following their normal
route, Strieber found himself driving
down a ramp that he had never seen
before. The ramp lead down to a 'sunken
highway' and Strieber commented to the boy that he must
have taken a wrong turn somewhere.

The unexpected road was completely deserted and as they
drove along it the two of them became more concerned.
Coming out of the tunnel, the pair found that they were
driving though a neighbourhood like no other they had ever
seen. The weather was suddenly sunny and the streets were
very wide. The houses had no windows and were set a long
way back from the road. They looked like big boxes and

stranger still, all of them had carvings of large serpents on their stonework.

BACK FROM THE OTHERWORLD

According to Strieber the place had a 'sinister' atmosphere and both he and the boy were feeling rather intimidated and scared.

Strieber turned a corner, then another, and suddenly with relief he saw an entrance leading back to the main highway. He drove onto it as quickly as he could. Stranger still, once they were back in home territory they found themselves on Route 80, about twenty miles from where they should have been. It had been only five minutes since they had taken their 'wrong turn', yet now they were somehow twenty miles away from where they had started.

After that rather unsettling experience both Strieber and the boy's father tried to retrace his route, but neither of them could ever find that strange neighbourhood again. It did not appear on any maps of the area, but both Strieber and the boy had seen exactly the same thing as their car drove through those eerie 'otherworld' streets.

DIMENSION SLIPS

The event happened at a time when Strieber was trying to get a better understanding of the visitors. Although he never claims so explicitly, it sounds as if he could have been 'slipped' into another dimension for a short drive through tour by his visitor friends.

But is it really possible to travel between dimensions? Researcher David Southwell has studied dimension swaps, (or 'D-swaps' as he calls them) for years and believes that under very rare conditions it can happen. He has collected stories from people who suddenly find themselves in familiar and yet slightly changed surroundings usually for only the briefest of times.

Parallel universes have been a regular feature of science

fiction television series for years, although the alternate universes visited by the Star Trek characters (such as the classic episode 'Mirror, Mirror') usually contain only minor variations from our own.

If the beings we perceive as aliens really do originate in another dimension then their home may well be something that we could never even imagine.

SEEING THINGS

During abductions and alien contacts there have been numerous examples of the beings changing shape. This has lead researchers to suggest that what we see as the aliens' bodies may not be their true form.

There are instances on record where witnesses to the same close encounter agree exactly on what the UFO looked like, but saw totally different aliens emerging out of it. One tall entity from a cylinder-shaped craft was seen as being female by the male witness to the landing, but as a male figure by his wife.

File No: 6529-77
Dateline: 27 October, 1974
Location: Aveley, Essex, England

During John Avis' abduction (see also Chapters 1 and 5 pages 7 and pages 52) he had time to converse with the aliens who seemed quite happy to explain to him the workings of their craft and other technological equipment. To him the aliens' technology appeared so advanced that it could almost have been magical.

Avis was shown some kind of 'visor' device which the aliens allegedly use to see in our world. He was told that the aliens use human eyes to see through, but sometimes 'when we cannot find suitable eyes we use the visor to change your lights to match our optic nerves'. The alien added 'It changes the impression that the static units on your planet see of us.'

BEHIND THE MASK

From the statement above it would seem that the aliens' eyes are so different to ours that they need help even seeing the people they want to abduct. What's especially interesting is that the alien actually says that the visor itself changes how the aliens look to us. 'It' creates the impression that we see of them.

The vast majority of abduction reports feature aliens with huge eyes which burn themselves into the memory of witnesses. Often a witness will remember with terror that they could not bring themselves to look directly into the deep black eyes of the creatures.

Could it be that the familiar features and large black eyes of the Greys are actually a mask? Is what we perceive as a face really a visor-device that allows creatures infinitely different to ourselves to interact with us as they visit Earth? It would explain why they all appear identical, and it would provide some logic for their lack of noses and motionless mouths as well as the absence of wrinkles or age lines.

BLINDED BY THE LIGHT

Although abductions are nearly always signalled by the arrival of a bright light of some kind, aliens themselves seem to be very shy of daylight. Abductions during daytime hours are so rare that it can be said they almost never happen.

Visiting entities have shown that they are vulnerable to light on many occasions. For example, the goblin-like entities that laid siege to the Sutton family's farm house (see File No: 3745–56 in Chapter 2 page 20) arrived in their craft at twilight. An hour later they emerged from it under the cover of darkness and scared the wits out of the Sutton family all night until they suddenly disappeared 'just before dawn' never to came back.

Although the aliens were completely unharmed by bullets fired into them at almost point blank range, they were frightened away by electric lights being turned on. The family soon found that bright lights were their only real defence.

THE EYE OF THE BEHOLDER

Author Andrew Collins believes that an aliens' appearance depends upon what we want them to look like.

In the early 1990s Collins undertook a two year research project into UFOs and their links to prehistoric sites (like ancient stone circles). He found that UFOs were more likely to be seen in certain areas (dubbed 'window areas') than others, and were more likely to be seen by certain types of people. Witness or abductees often have a history of other weird things happening to them in their lives. For example, they may have seen a ghost at some point in their past, had

lucid dreams, or witnessed poltergeist activity. They also tend to be people of greater than average intelligence.

Collins controversially believes that UFO encounters and abductions are caused by multi-dimension energy beings interacting with the mind of a human being. The energy being normally exists on a different dimensional plane to us, but under the right conditions it can interact with ours.

Quite rightly, Collins points out that almost all reports begin with a sighting of a bright white light, not an alien craft. Only after it comes much closer to the witness is the 'light' seen as a spacecraft. Frequently entities who are assumed to be aliens appear without the witness ever seeing a spacecraft at all during the encounter.

Andrew Collins suggests that once this energy being has made contact with a human mind, the individual then sees what they expect to see. In the middle ages people saw fairies; today it is Flying Saucers and aliens. While the theory is

complicated, it is an elegant way of explaining many strange phenomena.

Most abduction experts in the USA would strongly disagree with this idea. Investigators like Budd Hopkins are convinced that the aliens are real flesh and bone creatures who are here to perform experiments on humankind.

As with most theories, Andrew Collins' idea is almost impossible to test. It is a frustrating fact of UFOlogy that all investigators can do is sit back and wait for the next piece of the puzzle to reveal itself.

CHAPTER 8

Alien Lifeforms –
a Working Guide

So far we have looked at cases from the history of UFOlogy as well as some of the main themes that run through them. But what about the aliens themselves?

This chapter is a short working guide to the main extraterrestrial lifeforms that the reader may expect to encounter. These 'Alien Files' include details of the creatures' appearance, who witnessed them, and unconfirmed rumours which may or may not be true.

Study these files carefully because out of the sixteen entries one of them is a fake. It describes an alien type that does not exist. Readers are advised to take their time before deciding which file is bogus. The answer is at the end of the chapter.

File:0001-34 Name: Nordics

Description: These humanoids are about two metres tall with blonde hair and blue eyes. They have Scandinavian looks and are renowned for their physical beauty.

Witnesses: Nordics have been encountered by many witnesses and are one of the most common alien types reported after the Greys. Witnesses are usually charmed by the Nordics and feel safe with them, describing their manner as affectionate and all-knowing.

Nordics have been particularly busy in Europe where they account for one quarter of all cases.

Behaviour: The Nordics seem to have a calming influence on the humans they meet. They often speak about the need for peace in the universe and on Earth in particular. They claim to be here to extend the hand of 'galactic friendship'.

Unconfirmed Rumours: The Nordics are thought to be unhappy with the current activities of the Greys on Earth and want them to leave. Occasionally Nordics have been seen working with Greys, perhaps over-seeing operations, but even then the relationship does not seem to be friendly.

File: 0002-54 Name: Mothman

Description: A tall, frightening figure with huge batlike wings, webbed feet, and perhaps worst of all, no head.

Witnesses: Multiple witnesses in West Virginia, USA saw Mothman during a wave of sightings in November and December 1966. Sometimes Mothman is seen during a UFO encounter and at other times he will appear alone. His horrific looks guarantee that witnesses don't hang around for long. Terrified witnesses driving a car were once chased by the flying creature at a speed of around 75 miles per hour.

As well as the American visitations,

Mothman has also been sighted in Kent, England in 1963. A group of four teenagers, out one evening, spotted a yellow light travelling through the sky and watched as it disappeared behind some trees. A few seconds later Mothman came stumbling out of the undergrowth. The teenagers fled.

The most recent sighting was in Lothian, Scotland in 1979. Years later, the canny Scots - ever thinking of the tourist trade - put up a plaque to commemorate the event. Nine months afterwards the plaque itself was abducted, never to be seen again.

Behaviour: Swooping down from a dark night sky to terrify people out of their wits. Intelligent communication with Mothman has tended to be rather limited because of his lack of head.

Unconfirmed rumours: Although strongly connected with UFOs, perhaps Mothman really belongs in that category of weird creatures that include Bigfoot and the Loch Ness Monster.

File: 0003-78 Name: The Watchers

Description: Tall humanoids, similar to the Nordics, but more mystical in appearance and nature. Their technology is so advanced as to appear 'magical' to humans.

Witnesses: John and Sue Avis during their Aveley Abduction. (See Chapter 5, File No:6529-77 Page 52.)

Alien Abduction

Behaviour: At first the Watchers were passive observers as smaller hairy creatures examined the couple, but then they became kinder hosts, showing John and his wife around their ship.

Unconfirmed rumours: The Watchers are connected to ley lines and ancient Earth sites and have been interacting with humankind since prehistoric times.

File: 0004-05 Name: The Greys

Description: The most famous alien in UFOlogy. The Greys stand just over a metre tall and have pale white skin. They have large domed heads and big black eyes which dominate their face. Usually the Greys have no nose and their mouth rarely moves as they speak to abductees by telepathy. Greys tend to look identical, although often a witness will have a strong feeling that a particular Grey is 'in charge'.

Students of old folklore have long remarked upon the starling similarities between the appearance of the Greys and the descriptions of Fairies and Hobgoblins in legend.

Witnesses: Just about everybody. Greys and slight variations of them have been behind most of the important abductions on record: The bodies supposedly recovered from the Roswell crash were Greys. The famous case of Betty and Barney Hill involved them being abducted by small pale men with large dark eyes. So did the Travis Walton incident and many others including repeat abductee Kathie Davis. As many as 75 per cent of all new abduction cases in America now feature Greys.

Behaviour: Greys are the masters of the abduction scene, performing many more medical examinations than any other alien species.

There are a number of slight variations on the normal Grey with witnesses sometimes reporting a tall Grey who seems to supervise the shorter beings. Greys go about their work with a cold businesslike approach. If abductees question what they are doing they are told: 'this is important' or 'we have to do this' – which is of little comfort to the abductee.

Greys often seem to be observing the emotions of their human specimens as much as their bodies. On rare occasions the 'professional' mask drops, and a Grey will let slip their obvious fascination at human feelings and emotions. Perhaps such sensations are unknown to the Greys as a species.

Unconfirmed rumours: The Greys are the subject of many excellent conspiracy theories. The best says that after the US military recovered the remains of the bodies and crashed ship from the Roswell Incident they made a deal with the aliens. In return for advanced extraterrestrial technology, the US government agreed to let the Greys start their abduction programme experimenting on the world's population. It is no use writing to the President to complain; only the CIA and the men who really run the country know the truth.

File: 0005-29 Name: Reptoids

Description: Large hulking humanoid reptiles with four-clawed hands. Their eyes are reported as being slit-shaped (like a cat's) and golden in colour.

Witnesses: At least twenty cases reported from north and south America.

Behaviour: These sinister figures are spotted only rarely, but some witnesses believe this is because they are better at covering their tracks than the Greys.

Unconfirmed rumours: Could such creatures originate from a planet where dinosaurs did not become extinct as they did on Earth, but instead went on to evolve intelligence and eventually technology?

File: 0006-33 Name: Giants

Description: Over three metres in height wearing a silver suit and copper-coloured boots. The creatures have been reported as having three eyes; two white eyes and a middle one that is red.

Witnesses: In Russia during the month of October 1989, a total of over fifty witness saw a series strange craft in the skies and later observed six separate landings. The incidents all occurred in the city of Voronezh, south of Moscow. As well as the witnesses, evidence was collected on video tape.

Behaviour: In one incident a group of witnesses watched as a red spherical craft hovered over Western Park, before a hatch opened to reveal a giant as described above. The craft landed allowing the giant and a small robot device to step outside and take careful note of their surroundings.

Russian scientists examined the landing site afterwards and found unusually high levels of magnetism and imprints in the grass that would have needed a weight of eleven tons to create them.

Unconfirmed rumours: UFO occupants of giant stature are more common in Russia then anywhere else in the world.

File: 0007-04 Name: Praying Mantis

Description: A giant insect creature, basically a two metre tall copy of a Praying Mantis.

Witnesses: This strange and frightening alien has been seen on several occasions. In Maryland, USA in 1973 a group of four Preying Mantis aliens abducted a law student and examined him.

Behaviour: On another occasion a creature fitting the same description was found attacking a teenage boy. The boy was rescued with some difficulty and the being was chased away.

Unconfirmed rumours: Aliens who are observed as being insectoid by witnesses could in fact be ultra-advanced organic machines sent out as probes to explore the universe.

File: 0008-00 Name: Miniature Aliens

Description: Nine cm high spacemen who piloted a UFO about the size of a soup dish.

Witnesses: On 19 August, 1970, six schoolboys in Malaysia claim to have witnessed the arrival of the tiny ship and the ugly little creatures that emerged from it.

Behaviour: The small beings landed and began to set up some kind of signalling equipment. One of the schoolboys tried to capture the leader of the little aliens and he responded by firing a laser gun at the boy's leg. The other children ran away and later a teacher found the boy laying unconscious on the ground.

Unconfirmed rumours: Part of a wave of visitations by miniature aliens in Malaysia that year.

File: 0009-44 Name: Plant Creatures

Description: Roughly humanoid in shape, these beings seem to be composed of leaves and branches rather than flesh and blood. They move gracefully and have an air of wisdom and dignity about them.

Witnesses: On 21 July 1985, students on a school bus in Scotland noticed an orange light in the sky which appeared to be following their vehicle. It disappeared when they entered the local village.

The light was seen again later that afternoon by Peter Reich, a forestry worker carrying out a survey of the nearby Green Acre Wood. As the light came nearer, Reich began to see that it was a triangular-shaped craft with bright lights on its underside.

Behaviour: To Reich's amazement the craft landed and two beings 'like humans but made of plants' emerged and looked around. They spotted Reich watching them and engaged the bewildered man in conversation, mostly talking about the local wild life. At one point the tallest being turned to a nearby tree and asked it if the man was its 'server'. Reich told the entities he felt as if he had 'walked into an X-Files' story, but the creatures did not understand the reference and became confused.

Their speech and movement began to slow down alarmingly. They returned to their cube-shaped craft – the ten-metre journey taking them over half an hour.

Unconfirmed rumours: After this incident Peter Reich refused to ever return to that particular area of forest alone. He did go back with a team of investigators to show them the site of the landing. The team photographed burn markings and a circular depression where the craft had touched down.

File: 0010-65 Name: Fairies

Description: Small humanoids with thin limbs and bodies, sometimes sporting a pair of wings.

Witnesses: The best example of a fairy type of alien was observed by Jean Hingley at Rowley Regis as detailed in Chapter 6, File No: 67840-54 (page 63). Other beings of similar appearance have been seen around the world.

Behaviour: Bizarre and mischievous. The Rowley Regis fairies were one of the very few entities who deliberately inflicted pain upon a human - firing laser beams at Mrs Hingley.

Unconfirmed rumours: In terms of both physical description and their strange manner, this case adds weight to the theory that there is a connection between aliens and old fairy myths. The question of exactly what that connection is remains unanswered.
    There are three main competing theories:
1) That the similarities are coincidental.
2) That fairy stories are alien abductions that have been recorded in the past.
3) That aliens and fairies have a common cause and are the result of some interaction of environment with the human mind.

File: 0011-23 Name: Dwarfs

Description: These short entities stand out from modern reports of Greys because of their long beards and wrinkled skin.

Witnesses: On 4 May, 1969 in Brazil, two such aliens abducted a military policeman called Jose Antonio da Silva. He was missing for nearly five days.

Behaviour: The abduction began when da Silva, who was fishing at the time, was spotted by two of the dwarfs. The dwarfs, wearing matt silver suits, dragged da Silva to their cylinder-shaped ship and it took off with him inside. After a short flight, he was blindfolded and taken to a room outside the craft. The aliens spoke in a language that he had never heard before and about fifteen of the beings examined his fishing equipment.

A slightly taller entity with red hair and a troll-like face tried to communicate with him about weapons on Earth. Da Silva got the impression that they wanted him to act as some kind of spy for them and refused. The frightened witness was returned to Earth, but found himself 250 miles from where the creatures had interrupted his fishing trip.

Unconfirmed rumours: Rather worryingly, da Silva claims to have seen four human bodies stored on the craft – so who knows what the aliens had been up to.

File: 0012-55 Name: Giant Brains

<u>Description:</u> Large Floating Brains.

Witnesses: Despite being quite a common image in science fiction, entities fitting this description have been reported only once by John Hodges and Peter Rodriguez, the witnesses of the Dapple Grey Lane case in California (see Chapter 5, File No: 5395-04 page 46).

<u>Behaviour:</u> Peaceful.

<u>Unconfirmed rumours:</u> Acted as translators for other more humanoid aliens.

File: 0013-92 Name: The Visitors

<u>Description:</u> Whitley Strieber's Visitors are a variation of the common Greys, sharing with them their short height, large heads and big black eyes.

<u>Witnesses:</u> Other witnesses apart from Strieber have seen them. They have reported their skin is 'incredibly soft' and that close up they have 'a kind of musty odour'.

<u>Behaviour:</u> Mostly very friendly. They tend to act as teachers, keeping their distance in a mysterious and teasing manner. However, when confronted with questions regarding why they perform their examinations Strieber was merely told 'we have a right'.

<u>Unconfirmed rumours:</u> That they are gradually preparing the Earth for official world-wide contact by reaching out one to one to more and more people.

File: 0014-67 Name: Goblins

<u>Description:</u> Small green creatures about one metre high, usually having a large bald head and big eyes.

<u>Witnesses:</u> Goblins have been spotted in connection with UFOs on many occasions. The Sutton family in the USA spent an entire night hiding from them when creature who looked like Goblins visited their farm in 1955 (see Chapter 2, File No: 3745-56 page 20).

   Another famous Goblin alien was involved in the Ilkley Moor abduction (see Chapter 3, File No: 8499-06 page 31). Goblin-like aliens account for about 10 per cent of encounters world-wide.

<u>Behaviour:</u> Goblin aliens are normally friendly, although they can be rather mischievous.

<u>Unconfirmed rumours:</u> Like Fairies, Goblins are creatures that appear in both modern UFO reports and ancient folklore.

File: 0015-12 Name: Glowing Spectre

<u>Description:</u> A tall figure that glows bright green.

Alien Abduction

<u>Witnesses:</u> On 5 January, 1980, John Wilkins was woken at 5 a.m. in his bedroom by a green entity who seemed to be more like a holographic projection then a physical presence.

<u>Behaviour:</u> The entity told Wilkins that the Earth was in danger of splitting in half and that his race were working to save humankind. They had devised a plan to stop this disaster which involved their spaceships injecting cement into the Earth's crust.

<u>Unconfirmed:</u> The Earth is still in one piece so it worked - obviously.

File: 0016-33 Name: Men In Black

<u>Description:</u> Tall humanoids dressed in the style of 1950s FBI agents. They wear black clothes and are expressionless and unsmiling at all times. Usually they arrive at a witness' house driving a large black car. If the witness makes a note of the license number and has it checked out later, it is invariable found never to have existed.

<u>Witnesses:</u> In the 1950s-70s several witness to UFO encounters reported visits from the Men in Black.

<u>Behaviour:</u> These sinister agents interrogate the witness about their UFO sighting and then tell them to forget all about it and

demand they never mention it to anyone else.
Men in Black can behave in a threatening
manner or can be just plain bizarre.

The Man in Black who visited Dr Herbert
Hopkins in September 1976 looked 'like an
undertaker'. The being was bald and had no
eyebrows or eyelashes. He took a coin from
Dr Hopkins and as the doctor watched, the
coin went out of focus and vanished. The Man
in Black told him: 'Neither you nor anyone
else in this dimension will ever see that
coin again'.

Unconfirmed rumours: Men in Black may be
alien entities or they may be agents working
for the US government. Cases of MIBs have
declined since 1980, probably because
witness refused to keep quiet and even
reported the MIBs themselves, thus
generating more publicity.

Those different types of alien creatures account for well over
ninety per cent of all abduction and UFO cases across the
globe.

But which alien out of the sixteen different types was the
fake? Which report was completely fictitious? Was it the
ridiculous 'Miniature Aliens' witnessed by the schoolboys? Or
maybe the 'Glowing Spectra' alien, who was planning to save
humanity by injecting cement into the Earth's core?

In fact, both of those are genuine cases. So are all of the
reports – apart from the one containing the 'Plant Creatures'.
Despite their regular appearance in B-list science fiction
stories, there have been no reports of any plant aliens ever
recorded.

There are three clues in the report that give it away as being a fake:

1) The encounter takes place in daylight, which is very rare.
2) The alien craft changes shape. First it is described as 'triangular', then later it has become 'cube-shaped', before finally leaving 'a circular depression'.
3) Most important is the witness Peter Reich's reference to feeling as if he's 'walked into an X-File story' – an impossibility. The report is dated July 1985 – six years before the programme began in America.

CHAPTER 9

The Case Against Abductions

Despite all the eyewitness reports from around the globe most serious scientists remain highly sceptical about the phenomenon of alien abduction.

OTHER EXPLANATIONS

UFO debunkers have always been quick to forward alternative explanations for UFO sightings and abductions. Everything from low level clouds to the planet Venus have been offered as candidates for the objects actually seen.

A large percentage of UFO reports can be easily explained straight away. Most people know relatively little about the night sky and the objects that they can expect to observe. Falling meteors, aircraft lights, and space debris burning on re-entry have all been reported as alien spacecraft by inexperienced skywatchers.

With an active imagination, it is possible that almost any light in the sky could be a potential alien ship. Another explanation is that some sightings of strange airborne craft may actually be American Stealth planes being secretly tested over military bases.

However, even discounting the easily explained reports, that still leaves many objects that are genuine UFOs: genuine only in the sense that they are unidentified flying objects.

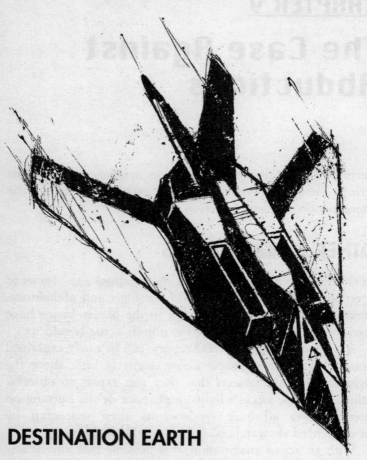

DESTINATION EARTH

One problem that UFOlogists have when trying to convince scientists is the sheer number of UFO sightings and alleged alien abductions. While such things are still very rare in the world population as a whole, over the last fifty years there have been thousands of reports of UFOs and aliens.

In fact, there have been so many that it sometimes seems as if a trip to Earth is a requirement of owning a spacecraft.

If you also take in to account that for every UFO that is spotted there must be another craft that visits the Earth and is never seen, then the numbers begin to be a real problem.

Half a dozen well-documented alien visitations over the last fifty years might seem like a good average for spacecraft stumbling across our green-blue planet by chance. But what we're looking at is a regular plague of alien visitors.

Why would extraterrestrials be so interested in humankind? And why would none of them announce their arrival to the world at large? Some might be from planets that have pledged not to interfere with developing worlds, but surely that would not apply to all of them?

SECRET PLANS

Abduction experts say that the aliens are choosing to work in secret for fear of causing a world-wide panic. Researchers like Budd Hopkins believe that the aliens keep returning to our planet for a specific purpose – their genetic breeding programme.

Hopkins points out that many reports describe aliens from the same race, - the Greys: small pale humanoids with large bald heads and big black eyes, who communicate telepathically with witnesses. He might argue that it is not a case of several different alien species making visits to our planet – but one species, the Greys, with a particular interest. In time, Budd Hopkins hopes that he will understand the Greys' plans through his continued use of hypnotic regression to recover memories from abductees.

TOO MUCH MYSTERY

Another major problem for UFOlogists trying to convince the world to take aliens seriously is the strange and sometimes just plain silly behaviour of the aliens during their encounters.

Perhaps we are wrong to assume that just because the aliens have the scientific technology to journey to Earth, they will also be mature and truthful during their contacts with us.

Sceptics have been quick to point out that, in general, the aliens' own behaviour on Earth does little to add to their credibility as a real phenomenon worthy of investigation. Frequently it almost seems that the aliens are working against being believable, and when you look at the things that they do and say, it is tempting to suggest that they do it deliberately.

After an encounter, witnesses find themselves having to report such bizarre and odd behaviour on the part of the aliens that it undermines their own case for them being real. If these beings have really journeyed here from another planet or from another dimension, surely they have a more worthwhile purpose than to hang around some lonely farm or country road and then leave quickly after greeting the first humans that they chance upon.

When alien beings make predictions about future events, they are inevitably proved wrong. Aliens always speak in half-riddles and never give a straight answer when there is an opportunity for pointless mystery.

Strange, illogical behaviour is at home in tales of fairy lore, but it somehow seems out of place when enacted by alien UFOnauts. At the end of the twentieth century, we expect visiting extraterrestrials to adopt a more reasoned and scientific attitude to exploring space and other planets – especially ours.

HOAXES AND FAKES

It is a popular belief among sceptics that a high percentage of abduction reports and UFO sightings are fakes or hoaxes. Scientists and the media like to portray abductees as money-grabbing people who will say anything for fifteen minutes of fame.

In actual fact, very low percentage of UFO reports and abductions over the years have turned out to be deliberate fakes. Whether abduction incidents are really due to alien interference is another matter, but most witnesses seem to be genuine and honest people. In the case of abductees, they are often frightened and scared individuals for whom fame is the last thing on their mind. Most abductees ask to remain anonymous and so are given a pseudonym when the case is written up to hide their real identity.

So why do people think that UFO reports are so likely to be hoaxes? One reason might be the series of alleged alien encounters that happened in the 1950s, in which the people involved came to be known as the 'contactees'.

One of the first contactees was George Adamski who co-wrote a book titled Flying Saucers Have Landed. Beginning in November 1952, Adamski claimed to have a continuing series of meetings with blond haired aliens from the planet Venus. The Venusians had 'mother ships' in orbit around the Earth and smaller 'scout craft' in which they landed.

At the time, Adamski became quite famous around the world as did the details of his trips with his telepathic Venusian friends. Among other incidents, Adamski claimed to have seen forests and rivers on the moon, to have walked on the surface of the planet Venus, and to have met Martians.

Since then science has shown all of Adamski's claims to be incorrect and the photographs that he took of the Venusian 'scout ships' have been exposed as rather crude fakes. Contactees like Adamski did a lot of long term damage to the credibility of UFOlogy and gave many scientists just the ammunition they need to ignore all reports.

FOR AND AGAINST

UFOs and abductions arouse strong emotions in believers and non-believers alike. Some high-profile scientists like America's Carl Sagan and Britain's Patrick Moore dismiss all UFO reports with venom, as if they were an attack on science itself.

Serious scientists with reputations to worry about are reluctant to involve themselves in this field, usually concerned that it will harm their standing in the scientific community.

After the publication of John Mack's book on alien abductions, he was investigated by a team from Harvard Medical School who were worried that he might have harmed the school's reputation. Taking the phenomenon of abduction seriously brought Professor Mack more criticism than anything else he had even done in his career. The silver-lining to that cloud was that he also sold more books than ever before.

While some scientists on both sides of the Atlantic are open-minded, most express their need to see proper hard evidence before they would consider the subject worthy of study. Scientists tend to harbour a sneaking suspicion that both UFO sightings and abductions are psychological, and take place only in the mind of the witnesses.

Indeed, there are many very solid arguments against abductions being encounters with extraterrestrials.

UNRELIABLE EVIDENCE

With sky bound UFOs, debunkers can always argue that although the object may have looked like an alien spacecraft, it was really a case of mistaken identification of a cloud or ball lightning. Alien abductions, where the witness actually claims to have seen alien creatures seem to allow less possibility for mistakes of that kind. However there are many other potential explanations.

Perhaps the greatest flaw in the evidence supporting abductions is that so many of the eyewitness accounts are collected by the use of hypnotic regression.

Experts disagree about how much this affects the value of the material. But where cases depend solely upon such testimony, we do need to be cautious about accepting the subject's recollections as being real events.

Most experts would agree that there are medical cases where hypnotic regression can be of great assistance in helping troubled individuals. The problem unfortunately, is that it is impossible to be certain that memories recovered under regression are real and not just fantasies that the subject's mind is just making up.

TELLING THE TRUTH

Few people fail to be impressed with the honesty and sincerity of abductees. They do not appear to be people lying or seeking attention. However just because a witness really believes what they are saying, it does not make it true.

In about one in five abduction incidents the abductee will have a normal and conscious memory of the abduction. In these cases, obviously, hypnosis need not be used and the problem discussed above does not arise.

The truth, as expert John Mack concedes, is that no one really knows how accurate hypnotic regression is and this undermines abduction reports – particularly as so much of the evidence relies on it alone.

LEADING QUESTIONS

Another flaw with hypnosis is that the investigator asking the questions may accidentally lead the subject into saying what he or she wants to hear.

For example, the subject, describing an experience they does not understand, might say: 'I see a bright white light ahead of me hovering over the road', the investigator then asks 'What did the ship do next?'. The subject has not mentioned seeing a 'ship' – only a light. But the investigator has made an assumption that the light must be an alien craft.

This small trigger might lead a subject in the suggestible state of hypnosis to make conclusions, or to recover memories, that are not actually their own.

SECOND HAND EVIDENCE

In the USA especially, investigators tend to find memories that support their own theory of how abductions work. This has lead some sceptics to claim that even researchers as well-respected as Budd Hopkins are in some way leading their regression patients in the direction that they want them to go.

Hypnotic regression is a difficult and controversial area. UFOlogy is a field of study where the investigators are often relying on second hand information. Reports from witnesses form the great bulk of the source material that UFOlogists have, and naturally they want to get as many details from these individuals as they can.

5) **When you are bored, do you ever catch yourself doodling alien faces on a notepad?**

   a) Never.
   b) Always.
   c) Umm, now I think about it, maybe sometimes.

6) **Have you seen a UFO or any kind of strange light in the sky?**

   a) Yes and there were other people who saw the same thing.
   b) Yes and I was the only witness.
   c) I've seen strange lights, but I'm not sure if that counts.
   d) No.

7) **Have you ever experienced a period of 'missing time'?**

    a) Not that I remember.
    b) Yes, every maths lesson is a complete blank.
    c) Yes, several times.
    d) No. I'm far too strong-willed to go along with any alien plans.

8) **The witness known as Philip Spencer met a little green goblin alien on which famous English moor?**

    a) Dartmoor.
    b) Exmoor.
    c) Ilkley Moor.
    d) Greenwich Moor.

9) **Have there been any UFO reports in your local area?**

    a) Yes, and I've followed all the cases carefully in the local papers.
    b) Not that I know of.
    c) No and there's not likely to be.
    d) Don't know, but I'll try to find out.

10) Walton Travis, the forestry worker who went
    missing for days, claimed to have been abducted
    by aliens similar to:

    a) Mothman.
    b) The Watchers.
    c) The Nordics.
    d) The Greys.

11) Do you watch The X-Files:

    a) Every week and you've got the best episodes on tape.
    b) If you're at home that night.
    c) Hardly ever.
    d) You've been living under a rock for the last year. What's
       The X-Files?

12) The country with the highest number of alien abduction
    reports is:

    a) Britain.
    b) Brazil.
    c) The USA.
    d) Japan.

13) When you're alone at night, do you ever look up to the
    skies and feel that there's something out there watching you?

    a) No.
    b) Sometimes, but it's my imagination.
    c) Yes, and it gives me the creeps.
    d) Yes and I'd love to see what they really are.

14) **Which of the following aliens have been reported to have three eyes?**

   a) The Greys
   b) The Giants
   c) The Plant Creatures
   d) None of them.

15) **Do you ever travel through the countryside at night?**

   a) All the time – I live in the country.
   b) Only during holidays.
   c) Never.

16) **Do you have a strong imagination?**

   a) Very strong.
   b) Average.
   c) My friends say I'm pretty unimaginative.

17) **Are you able to remember pictures and photographs easily?**

    a) Always, I've a really good memory.
    b) Not really, I'm better with words and numbers.
    c) I've a terrible memory for everything.

18) **Do weird things, like odd coincidences, ever happen to you?**

    a) Yes, but they do to everyone.
    b) No, and I'm glad they don't.
    c) Sometimes.
    d) All the time – my friends think I'm really strange.

19) **'Alien Implants' are used:**

    a) By humans to track down aliens once they are on Earth.
    b) By aliens who have hearing difficulties.
    c) By UFOlogists during investigations.
    d) By alien entities to locate the people they want to abduct.

20) **Having read Alien Abductions do you now believe in UFOs and alien lifeforms?**

    a) Yes, very much.
    b) I try to keep an open mind.
    c) No, but I could be persuaded.
    d) Definitely not.

Scoring System

Question number	Score for answer (a)	answer (b)	answer (c)	answer (d)
1	0	5	10	-
2	20	5	0	-5
3	0	20	15	10
4	0	5	15	0
5	0	20	10	-
6	20	20	15	5
7	0	5	20	-5
8	0	0	15	-5
9	20	5	0	10
10	0	0	0	15
11	20	5	0	-10
12	0	0	15	0
13	0	5	15	20
14	0	5	-5	0
15	15	10	0	-
16	10	5	0	-
17	15	5	0	-
18	10	0	5	20
19	0	-5	0	15
20	15	20	15	15

WHAT YOUR SCORE MEANS

0–110: You will be relieved to hear that there is little chance of you spotting a UFO or having anything else interesting ever happen to you.

110–180: You have a good knowledge of UFOlogy and an interest in the world around you. Definitely a potential witness.

Above 180: You have an excellent knowledge of the field of UFOlogy which combined with a strong and imaginative mind makes you a prime candidate for future sightings.

Readers with experiences to report are invited to write to the author:

Andrew Donkin
c/o Bloomsbury Children's Books
38 Soho Square
London W1V 5DF

IS YOUR
PET PSYCHIC?
TESTS INSIDE

Psychic Pets

SUPERNATURAL TRUE STORIES
OF PARANORMAL ANIMALS

JOHN SUTTON